The World of Yum SMOOTHIE™
Recipe Book Vol. 1

Author: Dustin Cromarty
Recipes by: Laurie Tissington, Dr. Becky Maes, Gabriela Lopez Vidal
Illustration by: Yanet Zamudio Castro
Colour and Graphic Design by: Gabriela Lopez Vidal
Creative Director: Frida Abaroa

Cooking with Monkey ©
Productions Corporation
™

Hi kids, my name is Monks. Welcome to the World of Yum.

This is my most favourite recipe book series in Yum Yum:

Cooking with Monkey - Yum Yum Smoothies!!!

The recipes in this series are super delicious, nutritious and smart. Think of each smoothie as an edible art.

A Smoothie a day keeps the rhythm in play. So, make sure you get all the good nutrition you need for regular activity, fun in nature, and a healthy, happy family!

A Yum Yum smoothie each morning will greatly help with this!

In this smoothie recipe series you will be introduced to some of my amazing friends from Yum Yum.

I have asked each one of my Yum Yum pals to contribute to this series of recipe books by submitting their most prized, personalized smoothie recipe.

I have asked my wonderful friend, Dr. Becky, to

comment on the nutritional health benefits of each recipe featured ingredient and to help with health tips throughout the series.

On each page you will find **Dr. Becky's Corner** where she shares helpful nutritional facts about important ingredients in each yummy smoothie.

Dr. Becky, MD, is a Board Certified Gastroenterologist, certified by the American Board of Internal Medicine. She is a nationally recognized expert on the treatment for what is becoming a global health crisis: degenerative diseases, inflammatory diseases, nutritional deficiency, and cellular damage. Her passion and life's purpose is to take wellness to the world through the power of education for children and their parents.

You will love her charm and grace as she helps us learn some very important facts about the nutritional power and health benefits of whole foods.

Smoothies are best when eaten with friends so please share this recipe series with all of your pals.

Tell them Monks suggested it!

Here's to good times, fun and learning with our pals in *Cooking with Monkey's World of Yum.*

Cheers big ears!!!

Monks

Dr. Becky's CORNER

Cooking with Monkey was introduced to me a few months ago and I was very impressed. I love its core values and vision to positively enhance the health, well-being and quality of life for children and families worldwide. As a physician, I've seen so many illnesses affect our children at a very young age. **It is my personal mission to help keep our kids lean and healthy through education and nutrition.** Because we live in a society of more and more "fast foods" that are nutritionally void we need to get back to the basics of eating fresh foods that supply minerals, vitamins, fiber, protein, phytochemicals and antioxidants that are crucial to our health. I am very excited about this smoothie nutritional book because these delicious drinks are loaded with nutrients that our bodies need daily.

This smoothie book contains some of the characters that you'll see on **www.theworldofyum.com.** The stories are full of fun and adventure with healthy living mixed in. You will find lots of other child-friendly ideas or tips online that will continue to educate kids and adults on the right food choices that enhance everyone's quality of life.

What could be better than cooling down with an ice-cold fruit smoothie? **These creamy smoothies are perfect for a quick breakfast, a healthy lunch, or a refreshing mid-afternoon snack;** all made with a bullet-type, easy to use and easy to clean blender. At any time of day, a smoothie can help you meet your fruit quota for the day! A bullet-type blender is very safe to use, but each family should take the age and ability of their children into consideration to decide if their child is ready to use it unsupervised.

I've listed some things that are easy adjustments to the recipes, whether you have any health challenges or are just looking to enhance your health and adopt a preventative lifestyle. When you flood your body with the right nutrients your body can fight off disease and illness. Great eating habits promote great mental clarity, energy, healthy skin and strong bones.

They are all gluten free unless you were to add in wheat or oat bran to these recipes.

These smoothies can be dairy free too – just substitute almond, rice or hemp milk, for cow's milk. You can also substitute goat's yogurt for cow's yogurt.

None of the ingredients contain HFCS (high fructose corn syrup) which has been linked to problems with sugar control and obesity and none of these smoothies contain yeast.

Greek yogurt has less sugar than regular yogurt or flavoured yogurt, but flavoured yogurt is a very tasty option. Yogurt contains probiotics which, as a gastroenterologist, I've always recommended, because they help to regulate our digestive

tract and are extremely important for our immune system.

Additional sweetener substitutions that I suggest include agave nectar (low glycemic) instead of honey, and xylitol (cavity fighting and fewer calories than sugar) or stevia (natural antioxidant and low glycemic) instead of white sugar.

Bananas also act as a thickener in a smoothie... and if you have bananas that are ripening faster than you can use them, you can peel a ripe banana, slice it into 1 inch pieces, freeze the pieces on a cookie sheet or plate and store in a zip lock bag. You now have ready to use ingredients for a smoothie.

If you use frozen fruit you don't usually have to add ice.

I like to stock my kitchen with my family's favourite ingredients, so a smoothie can be whipped up in minutes!

So, enjoy this recipe book and have the whole family participate in making these healthy snacks that give our bodies and brains wonderful nutrients.

Babo & Babu's
Blueberry and Strawberry Smoothie

Ingredients:
1/2 cup frozen blueberries
1/2 cup strawberries
1/2 cup pineapple/orange juice
1/2 cup plain vanilla (or another flavoured) yogurt
1 tsp honey

Preparation:
Put all the ingredients into your blender and blend well. Pour into glasses and drink with a straw.
For a thicker smoothie, add 3 ice cubes, blend in well, and enjoy with a spoon!

Makes 1 large delicious serving.

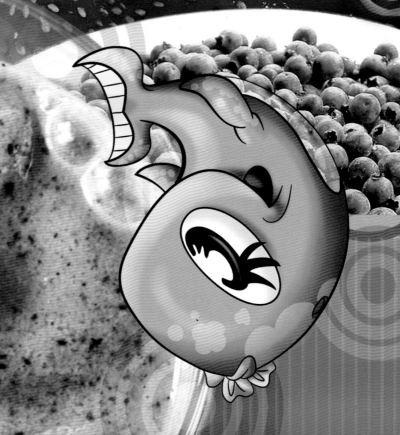

Strawberry fields forever!

Blueberries are sometimes called "Brainberries" and they rank number 1 in the world of antioxidant-containing fruits. This is mainly due to the presence of anthocyanin, a pigment responsible for the blue color of the blueberries. Blueberries are also rich in vitamin C. Together, these antioxidants keep your brain cells healthy and boost your immune system to help prevent infections. Blueberries are heart healthy, they are a good source of fiber and they are important to maintain good vision.

Strawberries are naturally high in vitamins and minerals and low in calories. Strawberries are high in vitamin C. They are a good source of potassium (which is a mineral that is good for our cardiovascular system) and contain folate, which is a key nutrient for the production of red blood cells. Babo likes more blueberries in his smoothie and Babu likes more strawberries in hers. Either way, this smoothie is a great drink to boost your body with excellent elements to support healthy eyesight, a healthy circulatory system, a healthy brain, hair and skin.

Bubba's
Bubble Gum Yum Yum Smoothie

Ingredients:
1 orange, peeled
1/3 cup frozen strawberries
1/2 cup vanilla yogurt
1/4 tsp vanilla extract
1 tsp flax seed oil
Add honey or agave nectar to taste

Blend well.
Makes 1 serving.
        Drink up and enjoy!

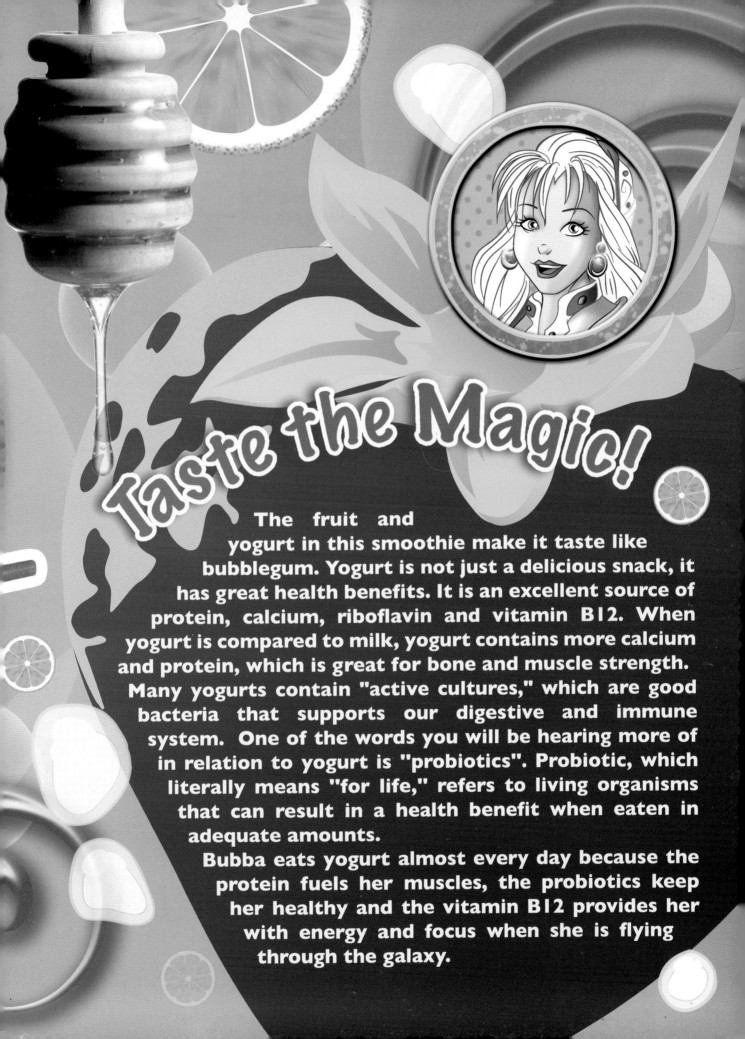

Taste the Magic!

The fruit and yogurt in this smoothie make it taste like bubblegum. Yogurt is not just a delicious snack, it has great health benefits. It is an excellent source of protein, calcium, riboflavin and vitamin B12. When yogurt is compared to milk, yogurt contains more calcium and protein, which is great for bone and muscle strength. Many yogurts contain "active cultures," which are good bacteria that supports our digestive and immune system. One of the words you will be hearing more of in relation to yogurt is "probiotics". Probiotic, which literally means "for life," refers to living organisms that can result in a health benefit when eaten in adequate amounts.

Bubba eats yogurt almost every day because the protein fuels her muscles, the probiotics keep her healthy and the vitamin B12 provides her with energy and focus when she is flying through the galaxy.

Baby Mic, Mr Burpy and Mrs. Tooter's

Rooti-Toot-Toot Smoothie

Ingredients:

1/4 cup crushed pineapple
1 fresh peeled apricot if available, or 1/2 peeled peach
6 medium-sized strawberries
1 banana
1/4 cup organic milk or almond milk
3/4 cup water
1-2 packets of stevia (optional)
1 tsp flax seed oil or ground organic flax seed
1 Tbsp vanilla protein powder

Preparation:

Put all the ingredients into the blender, and pulse until combined. Pour and enjoy.

Makes 1 large serving.

Pineapple for you!

Did you know that one pineapple is actually made up of dozens of individual flowers that grow together to form the entire fruit? Each scale on a pineapple is evidence of a separate flower. This delicious fruit offers many health benefits. Pineapple is high in manganese, a mineral that is critical to the development of strong bones and connective tissue. Pineapple is high in vitamin C and contains the natural enzyme bromelain, which helps us to break down and to absorb protein. Bromelain is also considered a natural anti-inflammatory, which means it can help alleviate pain, swelling or mucous in the body. If you have a cold with a lot of mucous, add pineapple to your diet. If you have an injury, such as a sprained ankle, add pineapple to your diet. Peaches and apricots are both very mild laxatives and, along with the flax seed (or oil), the pineapple and the protein, this smoothie supports good digestion and good elimination. This makes Mr. Burpy and Mrs. Tooters very happy.

Happy Happy Big Head's
THINK BIG
TRIPLE BERRY BLAST

Ingredients:

1 tsp Omega 3 Liquid Oil
   (I used a strawberry flavoured
   Omega 3 liquid oil, mmmmmm!)
1 cup mixed frozen berries
1/2 cup plain yogurt
3/4 cup almond or organic milk

Put frozen berries and almond or organic milk in the blender, and pulse until combined. Then, add the Omega 3 oil and yogurt and blend again.

Makes 1 serving. This one is so quick and easy!

OMEGA 3

Happy Happy Big Head

has a big head and he needs healthy fats like omega 3's for great brain function. Our brains are comprised of 60% fats, and approximately half of that fat is omega 3.

This means that nature intended the human brain to be "powered" by fats. If you don't have enough, your brain won't be able to run properly. Studies have shown that diets rich in omega 3 fatty acids can result in increased learning ability, problem-solving skills and focus. Omega 3 has been shown to help promote a positive mood and emotional balance, and can help us maintain healthy mental ability as we grow. Omega 3's are also great for our heart and help with inflammation in the body.

WEE MONKEY'S
BANANA PURE

Ingredients:

1 ripe banana
1 cup non-fat vanilla yogurt
1 Tbsp honey
6 ice cubes

Combine ingredients and blend until smooth.

If you like a tangy smoothie, use plain yogurt.
MMMMMM, good!!

Enjoy!!!!!

The Yummy Banana

Wee Monkey likes to swing from the "banana tree," but it is not actually a tree. A banana is the most unique of all fruits because, unlike any fruit, it does not come from trees at all, but from large plants that are giant herbs and are related to the lily and orchid family. Wee Monkey loves bananas because they are available all year and they are a great source of instant energy and potassium. Potassium is great for the heart and helps to regulate blood pressure. Potassium also helps our muscles contract and this helps keep Wee Monkey strong. Bananas also contain plenty of carbohydrates, which are the body's main source of energy. They are also easy to digest and taste great.

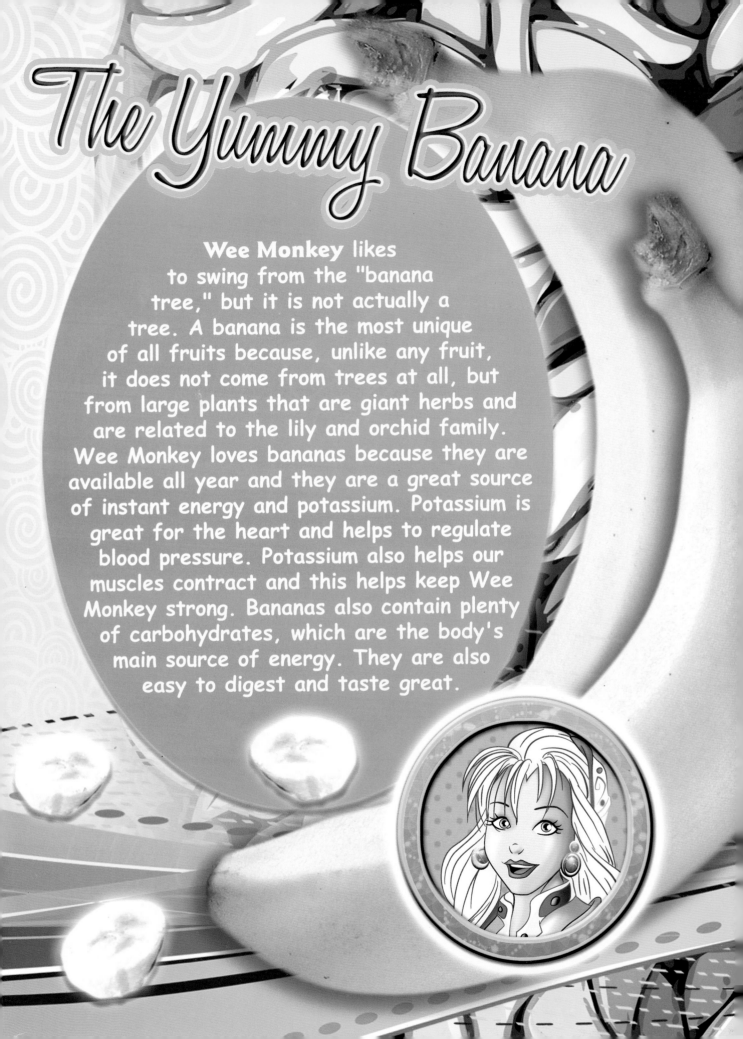

Love baby's
Hemp Hearts Smoothie

Ingredients:

1 Tbsp hemp hearts
1 Tbsp honey
1 cup orange juice
1/2 cup pineapple chunks
1 pkt stevia (optional)
3 ice cubes

Blend until smooth.

Makes 1 yummy,
tangy-tasting serving!

Hemp Hearts

The Love Baby has a loving spirit and loves to eat hemp hearts because these give her a lot of energy and a great attitude throughout the day. Hemp hearts are high in protein and essential fatty acids which supports our brain function. Hemp hearts are good for our digestive system. They also help to decrease cravings for unhealthy food. Hemp hearts are odourless and flavourless, so you can easily add them to just about any regular food and you'll never know they are there! Pour some into your cereal or oatmeal, add them as a topping to a baked potato or pizza or stir them in with spaghetti. The Love Baby puts hemp hearts in all of her smoothies.

Frank The Snaketank's
Buzz Berry Tummy Fuel

Ingredients:

1   medium ripe banana
1   tsp honey
1/2 cup raspberries   (about 8 berries)
1/2 cup blackberries (about 8 berries)
1/2 cup yogurt
6 ice cubes

Preparation:

Blend well and enjoy. Makes 1 large serving or 2 smaller ones. Delicious!!!

I Love Honey!

Frank the Snaketank moves at the speed of light and loves this smoothie because the berries, banana and the honey give him great bursts of energy.

The honey supports Frank the Snaketank's immune system so that he never gets sick. For thousands of years, honey has been often used as an effective natural home remedy to treat a wide range of infections. Honey has some properties that block the growth of certain bacteria to help keep our skin and body free from infection and inflammation. Honey has been used as a natural cure in first aid treatment for wounds, burns and cuts. You can also rub honey directly on the skin. Honey is also great for a sore throat. So, if you ever get a sore throat, mix some honey in warm water, gargle and swallow it down.

TETRA'S BURN TO LEARN SMOOTHIE

Ingredients:

2 scoops of natural vanilla whey protein or vegetable-based protein powder
1 tsp honey
4 slices of honeydew
1 tsp hemp and/or flax seeds
1 cup filtered water
3 ice cubes

Tetra likes to blend the flax seeds up first and then add all the other ingredients and blend together.

Makes one large vanilla shake. Many people, including athletes, love adding protein powder to their smoothies.

Honeydew

Tetra loves reading. He can read many books at once because he keeps his brain strong by eating a nutritious smoothie with his healthy breakfast every single morning. He loves the Burn to Learn Smoothie because the added protein gives him energy and focus. The flax seeds are great for his brain chemistry. Tetra also loves honeydew which is a member of the melon family. It is the sweetest of all melons when ripe. Honeydew has many health benefits because it is an excellent source of vitamin C, provitamin A, potassium, zinc, and valuable digestive enzymes. Honeydew is great for people who want to lose weight because it is low in calories and contains plenty of water.

Mrs. Tooters' Pink Fluff Smoothie

Ingredients:

1 cup almond milk (also try vanilla flavored almond milk)
1 cup coconut milk
20 cranberries
1/4 cup agave nectar
1/2 cup chopped pineapple
1 cup of ice

Blend well.
This smoothie is sooooo good!
Makes 1 large serving.

Loco-Nuts about Coconuts

Mrs. Tooters loves foods that contain healthy properties such as the good fats found in coconuts. Many people think coconut milk is the water inside the coconut. But coconut milk is completely different to coconut water. Coconut water is the clear fluid that you can see when you open a coconut while coconut milk is the substance squeezed from the thick white flesh (meat) inside a ripe coconut. Coconut milk is high in protein and also high in vitamins A, B and C. Mrs. Tooters also loves this smoothie because of the cranberries which keeps her immune system strong.

Ann the Phoenix's FIRE ENERGY SMOOTHIE

Ingredients:

1 cup of papaya
1 Tbsp lime juice
2 Tbsp agave nectar
1/2 Tsp flax oil
1 cup ice

Blend well. If you like papaya like Ann the Phoenix does - you'll love this smoothie!

Papaya is awesome for our immune system and for digestion. Papaya has digestive enzymes that help us break down and absorb the nutrients in our food. Ann the Phoenix loves flying in circles above Yum Yum because she is looking for more papayas to eat. Papayas are bright yellow or orange in color and are rich in Vitamin C, folate, and Vitamin B. In addition to fiber, papaya also contains potassium, which helps our muscles stay strong and helps Ann the Phoenix fly without muscle cramping. Papaya is low in sugar and therefore is excellent for someone that has diabetes.

PAPAYA

QUEEN MUNIE'S
BERRY BERRY GOOD SMOOTHIE

INGREDIENTS:

1 cup of frozen berries
(blueberries, blackberries,
raspberries and/or strawberries)
1/2 banana
1 tsp flaxseed oil
2 tsp lemon juice
1 tsp cranberry juice
2 tsp honey
8 ice cubes
1 cup water

Blend well.

BERRIES

QUEEN MUNIE loves berries because the deep color of berries is responsible for great health benefits. The dark colors (pigments) in berries are very good for us. They help our body stay strong. The blue, purple, and red colors of berries have been shown to be very healing for our bodies and keep us young.

B.B.'s
Super Lemon Breakfast Smoothie

Ingredients:

1 cup of frozen berries (blueberries, blackberries, raspberries and/or strawberries)
1 tsp flaxseed oil
2 tsp lemon juice
3 Tbsp cranberry juice
1 packet of stevia or your favorite sweetener
1 cup almond milk

Blend all ingredients together and enjoy. Makes 1 large serving. This smoothie has LOTS of flavor. B.B. thinks it tastes like the jam you put on your toast in the morning. It's so good!

Lemon may have some "sour qualities" but **B.B.** knows the health benefits of this amazing fruit. Lemon juice is also used in dental care. If fresh lemon juice is applied on the areas of toothache, it can help with getting rid of the pain. Lemon juice on gums can stop gum bleeding. It gives relief from bad smells and other problems related to gums. In addition, lemon can also be used in regular cleansing of your teeth. You can look for a toothpaste containing lemon as one of the ingredients, or add a drop of lemon juice on your toothpaste. B.B. loves lemon juice in her water first thing in the morning because it keeps her liver strong and healthy.

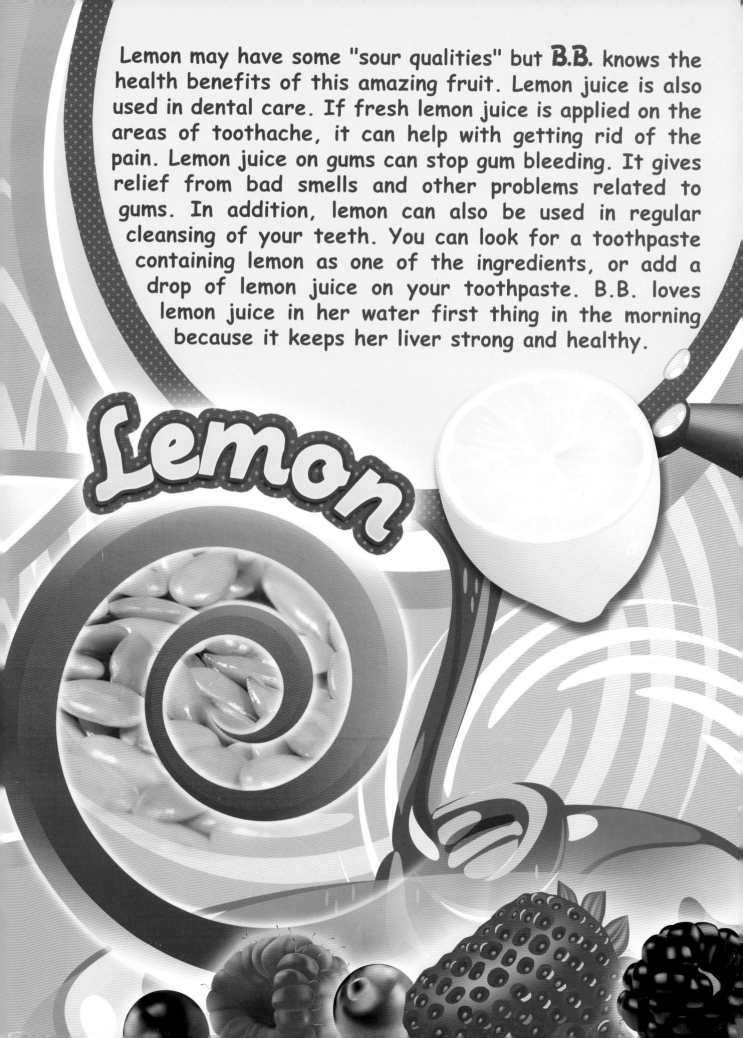

TIKY TAKA & UKU LICKY LAKA'S

COCO DINO-MITE SMOOTHIE

INGREDIENTS:

1/2 cup coconut milk
1 1/2 cups pineapple chunks
1 tsp bee pollen (optional)
1 packet of stevia or your
favorite sweetener
1 ice cube

Makes 1 large serving.
This is a great
tropical-tasting smoothie!

BEE POLLEN

When **TIKY TAKA AND UKU LICKY LAKA** are out having adventures on their dinosaurs they are especially curious about the bee hives they find. They have come to love bee pollen because of its many health benefits. Bee pollen is created by bees from the pollen of flowers. Because bee pollen comes from a plant source it has much more protein than any source from animals. Protein is great for Tiky Taka and Uku Licky Laka's energy and muscle strength. Bee pollen is also a great source of Vitamin B that provides great energy as well. This is why bee pollen products are usually known as 'energizers'. Bee pollen has been used for improving health and wellness since ancient times and was well known to the Egyptians, Romans, and Greeks!

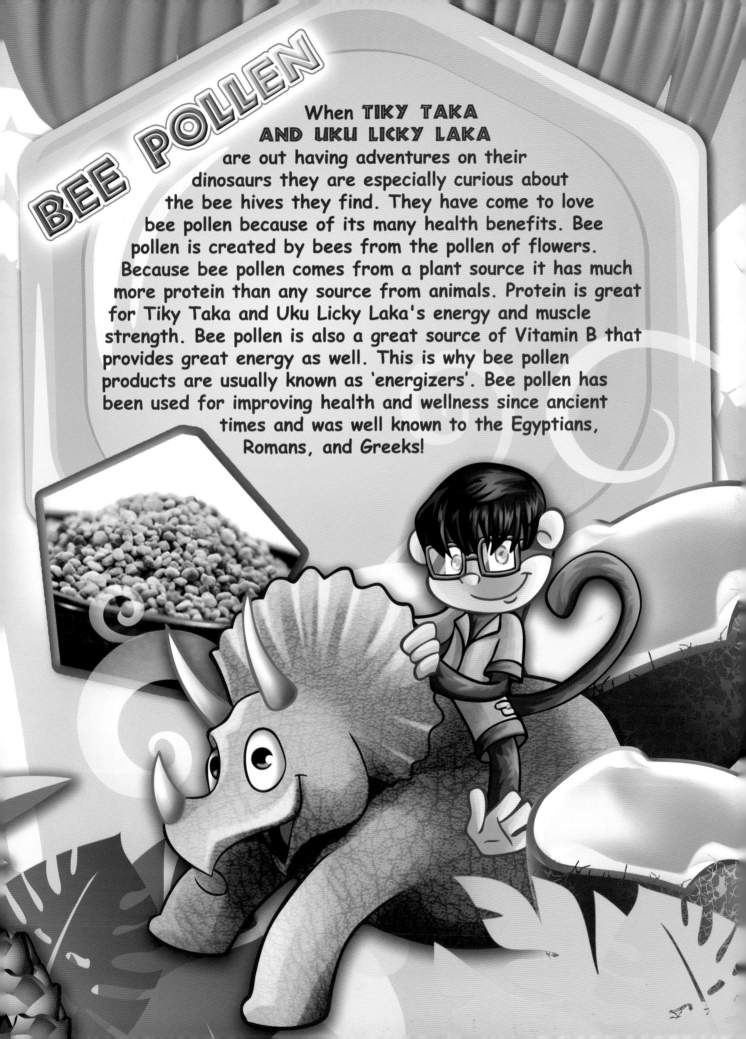

Um the Dragonfly's
Hum'n Buzzer Smoothie

Ingredients:

1/2	avocado – peeled, pitted and cubed
3	ice cubes
1/2	Tbsp agave nectar
1	cup almond milk
1	tsp fresh lemon juice
1/2	cup vanilla yogurt

Blend well. Makes a delicious creamy green smoothie that is jam packed with nutrients.

Avocado

Um the Dragonfly loves this smoothie because she can pick the avocados from the avocado trees she planted in her back yard. Avocado fruits are getting very popular everywhere in the world - especially in Yum Yum. Throughout the year, you can find avocado in your nearby supermarkets. Avocado is sometimes called "avocado pear" or "alligator pear". Creamy rich avocado is considered one of the world's healthiest fruits, because of its nutrient contents such as vitamin K, fiber, potassium, folic acid, vitamin B6, vitamin C, and copper. Avocados contain certain nutrients that are great for the heart and vascular system. One cup of avocado has about 23% of the daily value requirement of folate, a nutrient important for heart health. Avocado is also the main ingredient in guacamole!

LUDE E. CRISS'
PUMPKIN PIE SMOOTHIE!

INGREDIENTS:

1 cup of canned pumpkin
   - see note below
1 cup fresh or frozen
cut apricot (optional)
1 tsp of agave nectar
1 cup low-fat milk
1 pinch cinnamon
1/2 pinch of nutmeg
3 ice cubes
1/4 piece of banana
   - If you love the
   flavor of banana,
add the whole banana.

NOTE:

Since canned pumpkin pie
mix is already spiced, it
can be used instead of
the canned pumpkin,
cinnamon and nutmeg.

Blend well and enjoy!

Pumpkin

LUDE E. CRISS doesn't usually like healthy smoothies, but this is his favorite one. Pumpkin is one of the most nutritious fruits available. Pumpkin has healthy antioxidants that promote healthy vision and its vitamin C boosts immune function so we can stay healthy and energetic. Pumpkin is an excellent source of fiber, which helps reduce bad cholesterol levels, protects the body against heart disease, helps to control blood sugar levels, promotes healthy digestion, and plays an important role in weight loss. Nutmeg is a tasty spice that is perfect in this smoothie because nutmeg is great for the brain, heart, liver and kidneys (In small quantities).

Lily's Plum Delicious Smoothie

Ingredients:

1/4 cup frozen cranberries
1 banana
1 purple plum (pit removed)
1/8 tsp cinnamon (or more)
1/8 cup agave nectar
3 ice cubes
1 sprig of mint (optional)

Makes 1 large serving.
Very yummy and beautiful.

Plums

Lily loves plums, cranberries and cinnamon because they keep her strong and healthy. The health benefits of cranberries have been studied by scientists for many years. One of the best-known benefits of cranberry juice is the prevention and relief of urinary tract infections, but cranberries are also great for the cardiovascular system and may actually help prevent certain types of cancer. Cinnamon also has health benefits. In traditional Chinese medicine, it is used for colds, gas, nausea and digestive upset. It is also believed to improve energy and helps control sugar levels.

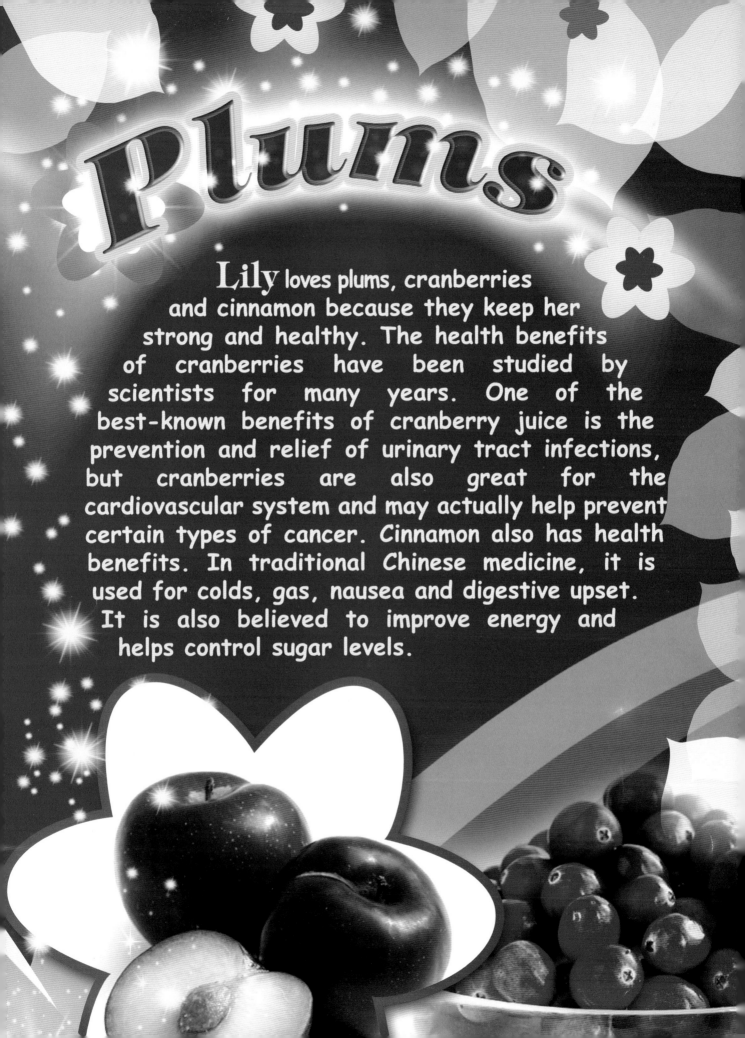

Look What Monks Cooked for you!

Colour your Moon with Bubba

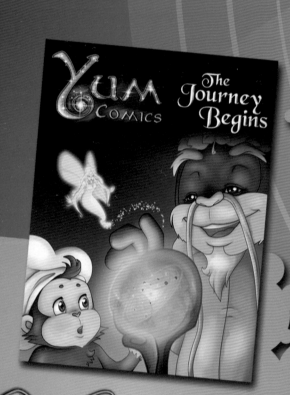

You can find these and other Yums in WorldofYum.com